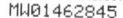

Presented To:

_____

From:

_____

Date:

_____

This book is printed in the United States of America by Joy K. Blair. No material contained in this book may be copied or retrieved in any manner for sale, but may be used in teaching and instruction for the body of Christ.

All scripture quotations in the text are taken from the King James Version, New King James Version or, Message of the Holy Bible. Used by permission. All rights reserved.

Copyright © 2016 by Joy Blair

ISBN-13: 978-1533430168

ISBN-10: 1533430160

"Wife Me Already"
Joy K. Blair

joyblairinfo@yahoo.com

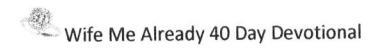

Wife Me Already

40 Day Devotional to Help Prepare You for Your Future Husband

Joy Blair

Acknowledgments

This book is dedicated to God, My LORD, Savior and King, who allowed me to go through such heart ache and pain in order to birth out this book and to perfect me, bringing me forth as pure Gold. Thank You Jesus Christ.

Also though I don't know T. D. Jakes personally, I want to thank him for pressing through all the suffering he had to endure in order to be used by God to help me through the hardest times and especially through this trying season of my life. T.D. Jakes, you are amazing. I thank God for you and your family.

I want to thank my kids, Joynisha, Sonja, Joseph and Gregory Jr. You inspire me to keep pushing through the pain and adversity. I do it all to make a better life for you all. Thanks to my beautiful Mother, Shirley, family and friends for loving and believing in me, I love you all. God has favored me with you all.

Finally, I want to say a special thanks to Curtis D. Jefferson, an amazing gifted man after Gods own heart, artist, brother and friend. Without you this book would not have been birthed out. You were used by God is so many ways. Thanks for being you. I love and appreciate you, thanks for believing in me even when I didn't believe in myself and helping me change my attitude and perspective on life as a woman of God. You are a blessing!

Contents

Prologue _____ 8

Day One: God is Preparing You _____ 18

Day Two: Who Do You Think You Are _____ 21

Day Three: Sudden Change _____ 23

Day Four: God Keeps His Promises _____ 25

Day Five: Humble Yourself _____ 27

Day Six: Don't Look Back _____ 30

Day Seven: God Will Restore _____ 32

Day Eight: Breaking The Cycle _____ 34

Day Nine: What If _____ 36

Day Ten: You Will Make It Through This _____ 39

Day Eleven: He Is Your Gift from God _____ 41

Day Twelve: Tame Your Tongue _____ 44

Day Thirteen: Get a Grip On Your Attitude _____ 47

Day Fourteen: Get a Grip On Your Flesh _____ 50

Day Fifteen: Get a Grip On Your Finances _____ 53

Day Sixteen: Stop Procrastination _____ 56

Day Seventeen: Stop Being Lazy _____ 59

Day Eighteen: Build Your Empire Queen _____ 61

Day Nineteen: Naked & Unashamed _____ 63

Day Twenty: Guard Your Heart _____ 65

Day Twenty-one: Flat Lined _____ 68

Day Twenty-two: Lord Help Me I'm Lonely _____ 71

Day Twenty-three: Bigger Than You Think _____ 74

Day Twenty-four: He's Asking About You _____ 76

Day Twenty-five: Patience for The Promise _____ 79

Day Twenty-six: Renew Your Mind _____ 81

Day Twenty-seven: Be Still _____ 84

Day Twenty-eight: Girl, Loose Him & Let Him Go ___ 86

Day Twenty-nine: Watch & Pray _____ 89

Day Thirty: What Are You Waiting On _____ 91

Day Thirty-one: Stop Complaining _____ 93

Day Thirty-two: One More Chance _____ 95

Day Thirty-three: Believe _____ 97

Day Thirty-four: Forgive & Move On _____ 99

Day Thirty-five: One Focus _____ 101

Day Thirty-six: Wake Up _____ 104

Day Thirty-seven: Ready _____ 106

Day Thirty-eight: Return to God & Relax _____ 109

Day Thirty-nine: Finish What You Started _____ 111

Day Forty: Ram in The Thicket _____ 114

Notes _____ 116

Prologue:

"Whose Rib am I?"

And the rib, which the LORD God had taken from man, made he a woman, and brought her unto the man.

Genesis 2:22

I gave my life to the LORD on January 18th 1998. I walked in the church one Sunday morning a sinner and left a Saint. The last thing on my mind was getting saved, well to be honest, it wasn't on my mind at all but apparently it was on God's mind (Thank You Jesus). Though I was saved and my heart was so full of love for Jesus, nothing else in my life was different. At the time I was living with my boyfriend and we'd just had a baby together.

The first thing that I did was tell him that we needed to get married. Each time I brought up *the marriage thing*, he went cold silent. It was so cold I would get chills. Eventually he told me that he did not want to get married. I told him that if we did not get married that he would have to go and he left. A month later we were married. I never asked God if it was His will for me to be married at that time because I didn't know better. I just wanted to make it right by fixing what I perceived as being broken. I was emotionally sick. I didn't want to be alone. I was so desperate for a husband and a relationship that I probably would have married anybody. He wasn't saved at the time and I promise you, I suffered for that decision. Six months later, after he almost died from accidently cutting himself while drunk, he gave his life to Jesus. We both were saved now, but not whole. We needed God to heal us both first before we got married. We hurt each other mentally, physically, financially, emotionally and spiritually. Just because we were living together when I got saved didn't mean he was the man I was supposed to marry.

Transparency with the Pain of Birthing

One day I was on the phone with a guy that I believed that would be my next husband. As we were talking I heard in my spirit *"Wife Me Already"*. It quickened me and I knew that it was a God idea. Immediately I told the guy my idea and he too knew that it was a God idea. I knew that it would be a book but I didn't know the suffering that was ahead of me. I didn't know the pain I would experience in order to birth the book out. Well needless to say, right after the idea sparked, things started happening that caused us to both shut down and seek God for guidance, direction and to remove anything in our lives that wasn't of God.

Our relationship was shaky because of both our pasts but the spiritual connection was strong. Once we both shut down to seek God, he was gone. I compared it to Enoch's story in the Bible. He was walking with God and one day he was not because God had taken him. God literally step in without a warning and SHUT IT DOWN. I was shocked and confused. I went through so much pain and turmoil. I cried every day and night because I missed him so much. I tried reasoning with God to bring him back to me. I was already praying and so I was able to hear God clearly and all He would say is **"Be still and know that I am God, the battle is not yours it's the LORD'S"**. I begged God every day to remove the pain and He said **"My Grace is sufficient for in your weakness My strength is made perfect."** And He said that I must drink of this cup. I was in such anguish. I had never felt such misery and pain in my life. I thought it was the devil tormenting me and trying to steal my blessing.

One day, God revealed to me that it was Him who shut the door and ordered this cup of pain and commanded me to drink of it. My first reaction was one of shock and confusion. I could not believe my Heavenly and loving Father would approve of this madness an allow me to suffer this way. Once I got over the fact that it was Him, I started feeling better because I knew that if He was in it, I was ok. He had me exactly where He wanted me to be. He separated me from everybody. I was in a prison of a pit. I was miserable, vulnerable and most of all extremely lonely. Throughout the entire process God told me to be quiet and to make sure I was quiet, He didn't allow anyone to call or text me. I had no one but God to talk to about my pain. I was in misery and misery loves company. God didn't allow me to talk with anyone because He knew I would have spoken against His will for my life.

God knew that I wasn't ready for marriage at that point. I needed a makeover. He had some major work to do inside of me. My attitude needed adjusted. My emotions were all over the place. My mouth and my confidence were unstable. I was afraid of dating this guy. I didn't feel pretty enough, secure enough, confident enough but I pretended to be.

I spent 20 years with my ex-husband he was all that I knew. I was comfortable with all my insecurities and imperfections even though I didn't like the state I was in while I was married, I didn't have to fix anything because I was comfortably uncomfortable. We divorced almost 2 years prior to me dating the guy, but he'd only recently moved out after me and the guy started dating. So there were lots of issues that I'd never dealt with. God had to shut everything down and prepare me for greater so that when I reached the heights He'd prepared for me I'd be ready for the blessings.

God does things decent and in order. I did not like the process of being on the Potter's wheel but I love the results. Through the process the enemy tried to get me to focus on me in a negative way. I started feeling as if the guy didn't think I was good enough, pretty enough or worth being his wife. Rejection tried to creep in and I tried to get mad at the guy and vow that I'd never talk to him again. God would not allow me to receive any of the lies of the enemy because it was nothing neither one of us did or didn't do but God who shut it down for His purpose. I try not to lean on my own understanding. I trust God because I know He's working it out for our good. I am now in a place of peace and joy. I am so grateful for the test because it made me stronger. I had the guy on the throne of my heart and that place is reserved for God and God only. In the past I never allowed God to be my only Husband but now I am in a place of learning how to love Him more and more. From this point on, no dating. I will wait on God until He say's I'm ready to be married again.

    I was so desperate for love because I didn't love myself. I've learned so much about God and about myself. This experience has been the best ever. I am so grateful to God for each tear He allowed me to cry. I thank Him for each time it felt as though I couldn't or didn't want to breathe. I thank Him for my storms and glorify Him for being in my storms with me. He told me that the battle was not mine but His (Exodus 14:14) and I believe Him. Surely He brought the enemy of my soul down to the ground.

    Your pain is your birthing place. Just keep pressing through the test and one day the pain will be gone and you will pass the test. Take it from me. Be strong, put on the whole armor of God and stand. You can do it. You will win. I love you.

God's Ordained Marriage

When God created you, He also created everything that you need in order to be successful in life. I believe just as God took time out to create Eve for Adam, God has the right one for you as well. He has someone special made just for you. God's exposing every counterfeit and all imitations must go. God takes us through the process of elimination. This is where He takes people out of our lives that either have already ran their course in our lives or the release of people that were sent by the enemy.

It will hurt when God starts removing people but it's for our own good. As you pray and stay on the right path with God He will present you to each other all in His timing and it will be perfect.

Finding Your Place in Singleness

God wants you whole and emotionally balanced. He wants to heal you of all your brokenness and the mental misconceptions that you have developed about having to be in a relationship. He has you in this place as a single woman so that you can learn who you are and who you were created to be. He wants you to realize that you are complete all by yourself.

He wants you to know that you have a life to live. He doesn't want you to wait on another person before you start living your life and fulfilling your dreams. God did not start forming Adam and in the middle of the process He stopped and realized that He had to make Eve in order for Adam to be complete. God made Adam whole before He brought someone along to help him build, create, nourish and replenish the earth. He created you whole apart from anything or anyone else. When you don't understand who you are and whose you are as an individual, you become desperate.

Desperation causes you to settle for less than you deserve. In this time of singleness allow God to heal you of all the hurt, pain, low self-esteem and to renew your mind from the lies of the devil that you've believed. It's your time for purpose. It is time to get to know you, the Whole you without apologizing for being great. If there are things about you that you want to improve, its ok to work on those areas while excepting and loving the real you.

Released from Prison

Understand that you are one of a kind and that there's no one else in this entire universe like you. Change your mind about how you see yourself. You are the asset to the equation not the deficit. You are valuable and unique. Free yourself to live. Free yourself to love. Free yourself to go above and beyond the limits that you have put on yourself and that you have allowed others to do. Make a decision today to change how you see your true value and worth by saying over and over what God's says about you. God says you are the head and not the tale. God says you are blessed and highly favored. God says that you are beautifully and wonderfully made. God says that you are made in His image and you are.

Embrace your greatness right now. Being in a relationship is a good thing especially if it's God ordained. But know this, you are a good thing first before the relationship. You are a good thing now. When the man finds the wife, she is already a good thing. You are already complete.

From Caterpillar to Butterfly

You are embarking on a path that you have never been on before. You're at a crossroad that's taking you to new territory and higher ground. You are on a journey that requires change. You must change, you have no choice. The caterpillar has no say so in the process to change. It's a part of its destiny. In order for it to be completely successful at what its created to be, change must occur. You have no choice in the matter.

You had no choice in the trials and test you had to face in order to get where you are today and you will have no say so in the one's you'll face for tomorrow. The good news is that you know it's working together for your good. Trust God and rest in Him. He is the orchestrator of your transformation and He knows exactly what He is doing.

Your change is in progress. Your wings are being developed so get ready to fly.

Conclusion

Are you in the process of a divorce or a breakup and your heart is bleeding from pain and despair? Are you in the process where you're continuously using different men just to get the attention and affection? Are you running from being single by dating different guys knowing that God wants you to shut all the communication down and set before Him in this season? Have you been single and faithful to God for years but still desiring a husband? Regardless of what stage of singleness that you are experiencing this book can help you.

    I've been there and done that and now I am using my EXIT route to help you walk out of pain into purpose. Take your time and read this devotional. Read it over as much as you need to. It's sweet, short and directly to the point. Also Meditate on God's word and allow Him to change you so that He can change your Ms. To Mrs. God wants to give you a miracle marriage. Go through whatever you must to get to where God wants to take you. Stop doing it your way. Surrender to God fully and your miracles will happen.

Wife Me Already

40 Day Devotional to Help Prepare You for Your Future Husband

DAY ONE

God Is Preparing You

And the LORD God said, "It is not good that man should be alone; I will make him a helper comparable to him."

Genesis 2:18

I know you may feel lonely, discouraged, confused and maybe as if God has forgotten all about you. But you press daily with a fake smile on your face pretending to be alright. The frustration of hope being deferred is making your heart sick. You imagined yourself married by now and living your dream life with your husband by your side. The clock is continuously ticking and you feel as though you're stuck and others are passing you by and waving their blessing in your face as if to say, *"Hey girl, Look I's married Now"*. You've written out the vision and made it clear on tablets and you read it daily but doubt and fear constantly creeps in because the vision is tarrying and not coming to an end according to Habakkuk 2:2-3.

You find yourself questioning God's word and His ability to perform. The enemy wants you to give up and throw in the towel. He wants you to doubt God's promise and settle in your desperation.

God is not concerned about your disappointment at His process and the time that it takes for Him to fulfill His word to you. He is more concerned about your development. The development of your character, integrity, your heart, your mouth, your attitude and everything that concerns you. He is making you into a Good thing so that Proverbs 18:22 *"He who finds a wife finds a good thing and obtains favor from the LORD'* will mirror you. He's making you into a wife that is comparable to what your future husband needs.

God has heard your cry. You cried out for the man of your dreams. The man whose designed by God just for you. Now you must stop resisting the cross you must carry and allow the pain and suffering to kill your selfishness and your flesh. I understand the load is heavy even Jesus didn't want to drink of His cup but He did.

He went a little farther and fell on His face, and prayed, saying, "O My Father, if it is possible, let this cup pass from Me; nevertheless, not as I will, but as You will."
Matthew 26:39

This is not a movement to be celebrated at this point but a death occurring within you. Of course it hurts, it's supposed to, you are dying to you. God's removing all of the toxics and waste out of your soul and spirit. Your ways must go and if this is the process that God has to take you through to get you to your destiny, then it must be done. It's God's will for you to drink from this cup. Go ahead and yield. Once you allow God to finish what He has started in you, then you'll rise from the death of this thing and receive your elevation, your crown, your man and everything God's promised you.

Promotion is on the other side of this pain. Just keep moving forward. You may have to go with tears in your eyes. You may have to go in pain and turmoil. It really doesn't matter how you go, just as long as you go. One things for sure, if you keep pressing on, the tears, the pain and turmoil will eventually cease to be. God will see you through this to your desired haven but you must press.

DAY TWO

Who Do You Think You Are?

For as he thinks in his heart, so is he. "Eat and drink!" he says to you, But his heart is not with you.

Proverbs 23:7

Take this time to reflect on how you see yourself. This issue is so important for you to evaluate. Do you think that you are single because you are not good enough? Do you think you're single because you are not pretty enough? The truth is you are single because you are too good and too pretty for just anyone. God knows exactly what you deserve. He knows all the hell and trauma that your heart has endured and He is not allowing you to go through those painful doors anymore. Your time is too precious to waste going in the wrong direction. He's standing in your defense removing every pretender out of the way.

Maybe you fear that because your past relationships did not work out, your future ones will not either. The enemy of your joy, happiness and your peace, wants you to feel as though you are worthless. The truth is that you are worth everything. You are worth more than your eyes can see, more than you can imagine. In this season of singleness, God is renewing your vision of you. He's changing your attitude about you and allowing you this time to get it together. God wants you to *"Get it Together."* Let go of the old hurt and pain so that you can walk in forgiveness and newness of life.

The Bible says that as a man thinks in his heart so is he. Whatever negativity you think or say about yourself is what will be. Watch what you say and monitor your thoughts. Upgrade how you see yourself and walk in it. Leave the past behind. Let the old you go as well. God has a divine plan and when you get married it will be for life because you will be new and you will be ready.

DAY THREE

Sudden Change

Then Moses stretched out his hand over the sea; and the LORD caused the sea to go back by a strong east wind all that night, and made the sea into dry land, and the waters were divided.

Exodus 14:21

God is preparing you for a miracle. Before I could finish writing the devotion for Day two I heard the Spirit of the LORD say ***"Sudden Change"***. God is going to change your life suddenly. In the book of Exodus, the children of Israel were on the verge of sudden change but they were too busy looking back at the enemy and listening to their threats. Inwardly they were afraid to let the past go because they grew accustomed to the provision.

The enemy wasn't feeding and providing for them because they cared about them but because God used them as a resource. God made their enemy's provide. The people were afraid to trust God and move forward without knowing how God would fix things. They cried out to Moses and Moses cried out to God and before they knew it they were on the other side of their problem. One minute they were standing in front of the Red Sea, scared, looking back, screaming, yelling and cursing Moses out, and the next minute the Red sea became dry land and they walked right through to the other side.

God is working on your behalf. It's all about His timing. When it's your time to be married, you will be. One day you will wake up single and go to bed engaged to the right man. One day you will go to bed engage and wake up married. God knows the right time and when the time is right, it will come to pass. You don't have to manipulate anything or run after no one. All you have to do is trust God. Keep feeding your faith and starve your doubt. Draw close to God resist the devil and he will flee. If you wait on God, one day you will experience the joy of God's ***Sudden Change**!*

DAY FOUR

God Keeps His Promises

*"God is not a man, that He should lie,
Nor a son of man, that He should repent. Has He said, and will
He not do? Or has He spoken, and will He not make it good?"*

Numbers 23:19

When God promise you something, it can get a little discouraging over time because of the wait. You must be resilient, relentless, full of faith and most of all patient. You must have a calm resolve to trust God regardless if there's no sign of the promise anywhere in sight. The promise comes with a process. There's different stages you must go through before obtaining the promise.

You'll be tried in the fire. Your faith will be tested beyond measure. Your mind, will and emotions will be under major attack. That's why it's important to cast down all imagination and every high thing that exalts itself against the knowledge of God (2 Corinthians 10:4-5). You'll feel lonely, rejected and forgotten by God. Everything around you will appear to be opposite of the promise. If you walk by sight, you'll doubt intensively and doubt is the enemy of faith. You must remain in faith. You have to continuously read and listen to the word of God because faith comes by hearing and hearing comes by the word of God. Stop every negative thought that the enemy brings to you. When you feel yourself thinking over and over again about how things will turn out, immediately cast your cares on God because that's a sign of worry. Cry out to Him until you feel a release of His peace.

    Ask God to forgive you for not trusting Him. Focus on Jesus and reflect back on all the things He's done for you in the past and remind yourself that He's not a man that He should lie. He always delivers just what He promises. Those that wait on the LORD shall not be ashamed. God will make it happen for you. He will bring your dream mate to you, He promised. Stay focused, keep your mind on Jesus and He will keep you in perfect peace.

DAY FIVE

Humble Yourself

For whoever exalts himself will be humbled, and he who humbles himself will be exalted."

Luke 14:11

Do you crave attention? Do you get upset if you are not recognized? Do you get angry when you feel like you are not getting enough attention? When you are in a relationship, do you get mad if he does not call you all day long? Do you get mad if he doesn't tell you that you are beautiful all day long? Do you get angry if he's not under you all day but rather out with friends? These are signs of pride. It displays your selfish ambitions. You want everything to be all about you. Recognize your pride issues and humble yourself. God hates pride. God is not going to give you a man after His own heart for you to break his heart with your dysfunction.

Whenever God deals with you about the spirit of pride it's because He wants to exalt you. He wants to promote you with the blessing He promised you but first you must humble yourself.

Before destruction the heart of a man is haughty, And before honor is humility. -Proverbs 18:12

God wants to set you free from the bondage of pride. He's going to do whatever it takes to starve that spirit of pride out of you. God allows uncomfortable situations so that eventually you'll die to that spirit and hate that very thing that's gripping you and blocking your blessings. Don't be afraid to humble yourself.

*Pride goes before destruction,
And a haughty spirit before a fall. Better to be of a humble spirit with the lowly, Than to divide the spoil with the proud. -Proverbs 16:18-19*

God wants your heart. He care's nothing about your offerings and sacrifices. He desires a heart of humility. How could you give God anything anyway? Everything you have, including every breathe that you take, God gave it to you. Humility move God's heart and draws Him closer to you.

"Heaven *is* My throne, And earth *is* My footstool.
Where *is* the house that you will build Me?
And where *is* the place of My rest? For all those *things* My hand has made, And all those *things* exist,"
Says the LORD. "But on this *one* will I look:
On *him who is* poor and of a contrite spirit,
And who trembles at My word. -Isaiah 66:2

We need to ask God daily to take the spirit of pride out of our hearts. We need to ask Him to do whatever it takes to humble us so that we can be pleasing to Him. We need to pray daily: *"Lord help us to love You with our whole hearts. Remove anything in us that's blocking our relationship with You."*

Fasting and prayer is so vital. Fasting humbles us. It's very important that we practice praying and fasting as a part of our walk with Jesus. If we desire to receive the blessings of God including our husbands, we must seek daily to be humble. We are no better than anyone else. If it wasn't for the grace of God you'll be doing the very thing that you see others do that makes you sick to your stomach. You are no better than anyone else. It's by Gods mercy and grace that you are able to enter God's presence.

If My people who are called by My name will humble themselves, and pray and seek My face, and turn from their wicked ways, then I will hear from heaven, and will forgive their sin and heal their land.

2 Chronicles 7:14

DAY SIX

Don't Look Back

But his wife looked back behind him, and she became a pillar of salt.

Genesis 19:26

Everything that God has for you is in front of you. You don't have to return back to your past for anything. You'll know when your future is close because your past will always try to evolve. All of a sudden here comes the phone calls, text messages, invitations and all kinds of foolish distractions emerging from your past. That's why it's so important to keep a vision of your future in front of you. It's been said that if you don't have a future, you'll always return back to your past.

The message of *"Not Looking Back"* is so serious that Jesus in one of His sermons went all the way back to Genesis and brought up this topic. In Luke 17:32 Jesus said, ***"Remember Lots wife"***. Jesus knows that there's nothing in your past but heart ache and pain. He has a better plan for your life. His plan is greater than you can imagine. Isaiah 55:8-9 say's

"For My thoughts are not your thoughts, Nor are your ways My ways," says the LORD. "For as the heavens are higher than the earth, so are My ways higher than your ways, And My thoughts than your thoughts."

You've cried and prayed, prayed and cried and finally God delivered you out of that bad relationship or that situation and now you are looking back. Why? What are you looking back for? You were miserable. God has released you from your past. There's nothing back there for you. Looking back indicates that you want your past more than your future. If you go back, it'll paralyze you. You'll become stuck, just like "Lot's wife".

I understand that things may not be moving as fast as you desire. It may seem as if things are not moving at all but know this, God is working behind the scene and He's working on your behalf getting things done in your favor. James 1:2-3 say's

"Count it all joy when you are faced with various trials, knowing that the testing of your faith produces patience. But let patience have its perfect work, that you may be perfect and complete, lacking nothing."

Allow God to have His way with your transformation no matter how long it takes Him to complete His work and always remember, that God makes no mistakes, His timing is perfect.

DAY SEVEN

God Will Restore

"So I will restore to you the years that the swarming locust has eaten, The crawling locust, the consuming locust, And the chewing locust, My great army which I sent among you. You shall eat in plenty and be satisfied, and praise the name of the LORD your God, who has dealt wondrously with you; And My people shall never be put to shame.

Joel 2:25-26

You are in for a great awakening. God is going to restore everything that the enemy has stolen from you. Whatever it is that you lost get ready for it to be replaced. The devil meant it for bad but God will use it for your good. Don't fret anymore over your loss. Stop crying over your past as if God does not have an amazing future in store for you.

Don't live dissimulated another day as if God knew nothing about your trouble. He saw every attack, every battle, everything that you lost before it ever happened. He already had a plan in effect from the foundation of the world. He took in consideration your entire journey and incorporated all your pain and losses as part of His purpose. Your pain is for a purpose. When a woman is pregnant and having labor pains, though it hurts so bad, she knows that the pain has purpose. Right now you are pregnant, your water broke and now it's time to push. All of your hurt, struggle, rejection and pressure are signals that you are in labor. It's time to give birth to your blessings.

God's about to restore relationships on major levels. The relationships in the past can't come close to the new ones that God is sending to you. God is giving you restored hope, new blessings, new opportunities and so much more. Do not shed another tear of sadness over what you've lost. Allow God to heal your heart so that you can feel again. Open yourself up for God to pour into you. Receive all that God has for you. From this day forward let your tears be tears of Joy. Get ready for restoration.

DAY EIGHT

Breaking The Cycle

"The LORD our God spoke to us in Horeb, saying: 'You have dwelt long enough at this mountain."

Deuteronomy 1:6

I realize that we oftentimes look to others to love us or make us feel valuable or worthy. We run from God, the One and only person that truly loves us, to try to find love outside of Him. What I am learning is that with all the running, we are really running from ourselves.

So many women find themselves in the same situation of a mess over and over again. Looking for love in all the wrong places with all the wrong motives. She's so desperate for love that she's willing to settle for the first person she feels has a little potential, knowing within her heart that he's not the one. Entering relationships without consulting God (Our Father). She finds herself praying, trying to get God to be incompliance with her unhealthy decision as if He's not sending her multiple warning signs that *"He's not the one."*

Now she opens herself up for love to only find herself hurt and broken all over again. Now she has another bad relationship added to the list. Married and now she's lonely as ever. Finally waking up to only find herself in divorce court struggling to hold on to her sanity.

Stop opening yourself up to different men. This space, at this time in your life is reserved for you and God only. This is a place where He has ordained you to seek after, find, worship and love Him and Him only. When the time is right, He'll open the door and allow the right man to come into your life. You won't have to worry about the pain and misconceptions, distraction and lies because God only has the best for you.

When you cut off all the wrong men, your peace will be like a river. You won't have to worry if he's real or not or try to figure out his motives. To top it off, you won't have to go through the withdraw of not receiving his texts, calls, pictures and whatever else that has to be deleted from your soul's memory bank. Enough is enough. This is the END. This is the end of doing it backwards. It's not your job to go looking for love. It's his job to come looking for you.

You are special, you are the blessing, you are the good thing. His job is to find God and God will lead him to you. *He who finds a wife finds a good thing, and obtains favor from the Lord.*

-Proverbs 18:22

DAY NINE

What If

If it be so, our God whom we serve is able to deliver us from the burning fiery furnace, and he will deliver us out of thine hand, O king. But if not, be it known unto thee, O king, that we will not serve thy gods, nor worship the golden image which thou hast set up.

Daniel 3:17-18

It's so easy to get excited and amped up about your future husband and that's a good thing. But allow me to cut in on your expectation for just a minute and ask you a few questions. What if God doesn't bless you with a husband? What if His plan for you leaves you without a man in your life? What if God's plan includes you and Him only? What if He does not want to share you with anyone else?

If this is the case, be honest with yourself, how would it make you feel? Would you feel sad and down? Would you feel disappointed? To be honest with you, I am only asking you these questions because God asked me.

The first emotion I had was a sad one. I can remember dropping my head and my heartbeat slowed down as well. I felt as though I would be missing out on something great. I felt as though I was being cheated. I love God and I know that He's my first husband, but I wanted my natural husband too.

To be honest, at that moment I wanted my natural man more. Once I came to myself, I immediately felt bad because I didn't want to hurt God. I asked Him to please forgive me. I remember reading in the Old Testament of the Bible, when the children of Israel wanted a king because other nations had kings. Samuel reminded them that God was their King. But they didn't want God, they wanted a man, a king that they could see. The situation really bothered God. He was hurt because they wanted to trade Him, after all He'd done for them. He loved them so much but the love wasn't reciprocated. I never forgot that.

It always makes me feel bad when I find myself sad an unhappy because of what I don't have. Instead I should be grateful for the blessings He's bestowed upon me. I realize that it's an honor for God to choose us as His special treasure and for Him to shower us with His love, grace and mercy daily.

He has such an amazing plan for our lives and as our covering, He's going to make sure we are protected. He's not going to allow just any man to rule over you, that's why the other relationships did'nt amount to anything. You are deer and very delicate to God and that's why He doesn't trust just any one to handle you. That's an awesome thing. My prayer is that you'll be willing to surrender all and follow Him regardless of where it leads you. I really believe that if you love on God and be willing to be all His, He'll make sure you reap the love that you've sown in an extraordinary way. If you are willing to go all the way with God, He'll speed up the process and your wait won't be long. Girl, your king is coming!

DAY TEN

You Will Make It Through This

No weapon formed against you shall prosper, And every tongue which rises against you in judgment You shall condemn. This is the heritage of the servants of the LORD, And their righteousness is from Me,"
Says the LORD.

Isaiah 54:17

Sometimes life can be so challenging making it hard to move forward. It may seem as though every door is shut, every window locked and all odds against you. You may feel as though you're all alone and no one cares for you. You may be in a place of rejection. You may be in a place where you're being attacked with lies. You may be in a place where your name is being discredited. You may be in a place where you feel unappreciated and used. You may be in a place that you know you've outgrown and it is time to move on but you are afraid.

Where ever you are at this time in your life, God knows and see's everything you're experiencing and most of all He cares and He's right there with you. All the forces of hell could not stop God from being in your struggle with you. The truth is that if God wasn't in the trails with you, you couldn't survive. God is with you and eventually He will bring you out. I know it seems as though you won't make it through and that it's never ending. But one day you will be on the other side of this test and you will see that all of the hardships that you've experienced worked together for your good.

You need each and every one of these obstacles because of where God is taking you. He's building your strength, endurance, character and stamina. He's perfecting you. He's making your skin thick so that you won't be easily broken or offended ever again. He's preparing you for something so far greater than you can imagine. Your eyes have not seen and your ears have not heart, your heart can't imagine what God has in store for you because you love Him. God has something special waiting for you after this. Hang in there.

But as it is written, Eye hath not seen, nor ear heard, neither have entered into the heart of man, the things which God hath prepared for them that love him.

1 Corinthians 2:9

DAY ELEVEN

He Is Your Gift from God

Wait on the LORD, and keep his way, and he shall exalt thee to inherit the land: when the wicked are cut off, thou shalt see it.

Psalms 37:34

God's promises are sacred and He never makes promises that He doesn't intend on keeping. He can't lie. He promised you the land. In this case the land is your Husband, your king, your ordained mate, your best friend, your man. A man after His own heart. He said that He would give you the desires of your heart. After all the heart break and heart ache you've encountered and you still have the desire for love, a desire to get married, a desire to share yourself with that special someone, you know that's God's grace and mercy.

I know this is true because if you didn't want your man, you would not be reading this book. God has taken into consideration all you've endured and He has someone tailor made just for you. He knows your heart and as long as you remain open and yielded to Him, He will bring you exactly what He promised.

*Delight yourself also in the L*ORD*,
And He shall give you the desires of your heart.*

Psalms 37:4

In between God making the promise and you receiving it is called *"Process".* This is where your faith will be tested and tried. This is where doubt and fear dwells. God ordained the process so that He can make you better not bitter. Before He presents you to your future husband, He has to prepare you. He has to cut off all your enemies including your inner enemies. God wants to purge you from every spirit and demonic stronghold that you're in bondage to, so that you won't have to take that mess into your marriage and find yourself in divorce court.

    You must die to pride and all selfishness. God don't want to give you the land so that you lose it. If He did give it to you too soon, it'll set you up for failure. He wants to deal with the hidden areas of your heart. The parts that you don't want anyone to know about. Those are the areas that God's after. God does not just want the unclean spirits to lay dormant, He wants them destroyed. No more flesh standing in the way of your happiness.

    God wants you to love your **husband**. You're to crown him, not cut him and as long as you keep those enemies alive, they'll continue to ruin your life and make a mockery out of you. *Therefore put to death your members which are on the earth: fornication, uncleanness, passion, evil desire, and covetousness, which is idolatry. Because of* *these things the wrath of God is coming upon the sons of disobedience, in which you yourselves once walked when you lived in them. But now you yourselves are to put off all these: anger, wrath, malice, blasphemy, filthy language out of your mouth -Colossians 3:5-8.*

Once God finishes with you. He will exalt you and promote you to inherit your promise. He's unblocking all the traps, and cutting off your enemies and you will see it with your own eyes and soon you will embrace your blessing.

DAY TWELVE

Tame Your Tongue

Put away from thee a froward mouth, and perverse lips put far from thee.

Proverbs 4:24

During this time of processing, God is working on the weak areas of your life. Do you have a problem with your mouth? Do you find yourself saying things that you regret later? Do you have an attitude problem? Do you have to bite your lip to keep from letting somebody have a piece of your mind? If you've answered yes to any of these questions, God is after your tongue. He wants you to learn how to discipline yourself to say what's right even when you feel wronged. You must control your tongue.

Taking control of your mouth is a choice. The fruit that you are reaping now is the product of the seeds that you've sown. If you are not happy with your crop thus far, change the seed that you are putting in the field. Change your words. Are you single because you have a bad attitude and an independent uncontrollable tongue? Do your kids or anyone else hate to be around you because you can't seem to find balance in your frustration? The Bible speaks of the tongue being a very small member but it boasted great things and starts big fires (James 3:5). Is your tongue starting dangerous fires in your life? Are you hurting yourself, your kids, your finances, your health and relationships all because you won't take time out to discipline the words that are coming out of your mouth or because you value your pride to much to shut up? Are you cursing the land instead of blessing it?

It's time out for reading the Bible every day, going to church and still not changing and being transformed into the image of Jesus. It's time to die to our own selfish ways and display Christ Jesus. Jesus is our focus and our aim should be to please Him. Is He pleased with your attitude? Are you putting in the effort to make the proper changes needed? If you know that your tongue is dangerous, you need to make a strategic effort to change it. In the process you must be patient with yourself.

Pray and ask God to help you change your attitude. Start a fast, a Daniel fast, where you eat only fruit and vegetables for at least 21 days. Always pray and ask God which fast He's chosen for you to do and do it. God has a chosen fast just for you. It's designed to break the yokes of bondage off you, so that you can be successful in life. *Is not this the fast that I have chosen? to loose the bands of wickedness, to undo the heavy burdens, and to let the oppressed go free, and that ye break every yoke? -Isaiah 58:6*

Find scriptures in the Bible pertaining to your tongue and meditate on them over and over again during your 21 day fast. Also practice being quiet. If you know you have nothing good to say, **"Shut Up", just be quiet**. Continuously do this until you see change in your actions and behavior and most of all in your life. The Bible says that life and death are in the power of the tongue and those who love it will eat its fruit -Proverbs 18:21. God wants you to be ready when your mate comes. This is a part of His process for you. So humble yourself and do His will. After all, Queen, It's for your own good. Girl, you got this. I love you.

DAY THIRTEEN

Get A Grip On Your Attitude

Complain if you must, but don't lash out. Keep your mouth shut, and let your heart do the talking. Build your case before God and wait for his verdict.

Psalms 4:4-5 (MSG)

I know that we just finished talking about the tongue and spoke on the attitude as well. Your attitude will break you or make you. You can be one of the prettiest women in the world and have a bad attitude and it makes you ugly. It takes away from the attributes of who you really are. Beauty is not just an outer quality it's an inside masterpiece. Inner beauty is so bright that it shines through the body. It illuminates the soul and everybody can see it. We put so much value on our hips and lips that we fail to see what true beauty is. We invest more time in temporary stamina then in the things that really matter.

You should focus more on dressing up your spirit with God's word then on your lipstick and outfit. God's word is a mirror and it makes adjustments accordingly. If you need work done, it will show you exactly where and what needs to be done and how to solve the problem. If your attitude stinks, God will clarify that as you read His word and help you fix it if you'll follow His leading. You don't need plastic surgery all you need is a Bible and a willing, obedient and open heart. God will make you a true beauty indeed because it's His will for your life.

    God wants to dig deep within you and repair all the broken pieces. You have to allow Him to do so. He wants to beautify you from the inside out, not accidentally but on purpose for His purpose. Your future husband need you to be fixed, you both have major work to do for God's Kingdom which include healing the broken hearted. Your heart doesn't need to be broken.

    I am reminded of Queen Esther and how she was next in line for her blessing. Her husband was a major benefit from her obedience to the plan and will of God. She had no clue how close her blessing was. She was simply focused on God. The wife before her Queen Vashti was, on the other hand, too comfortable in her relationship with her husband that she lost respect for him. She had a bad attitude, unwilling spirit and she wasn't even thinking of changing.

    She was so prideful in her outer beauty that she didn't think she could be replaced. She never thought to secure her position with a willing spirit. One day her kingdom came tumbling down and she lost everything. Her beauty could no longer hold her position as the king's wife.

She was deceived and eventually replaced. Deception will cause you to be replaced. She put her trust in her looks and her looks let her down. You must put your trust in God. God is the only One who has the power to raise up one and put down another. Esther had the right foundation for her blemishes. Her beauty was built on the ROCK, Jesus Christ, the One and only KING. She had her faith and trust in God and at the right time God exalted her and made her Queen because her heart was right.

Don't get me wrong, I am not saying not to take care of your physical man, that's a must. Esther had to go through stages of beautification and purification before she could even go before the King. What I am saying is not to neglect your heart. Get your heart right. Develop a gentle and quiet spirit which is incorruptible beauty. With a heart after God's own heart, you can't go wrong. God holds the hearts of kings in His hand and He turns the heart whichever way He desires. Get in position so that God can favor you and turn the right kings heart toward you. GET IT TOGETHER. Your king is coming, Queen.

DAY FOURTEEN

Get A Grip On Your Flesh

For this is the will of God, even your sanctification, that ye should abstain from fornication

1 Thessalonians 4:3

LORD Jesus we need your help with this right here. I am a firm believer that once you give your life to God that you are no longer yours and that you belong to Him totally. Sexual sin is no longer acceptable. Now I know and understand that we are not perfect but we should not put ourselves in situations that tempt us to commit adultery or sexual sin. So many women lower their standards, leave their post and compromise, risking everything for a man who could care less but because of desperation secretly screaming **"Wife Me Already"**.

Thank God for shut doors. Thank God for His mercy and grace. We need Jesus every hour of the day. It's so easy to say what you will and will not do. It's easy to say that you won't have sex until you get married if you are not dating anyone at the time. But once you start dating a guy that you are crazy about and he could be a potential husband, talk to me then. God warns us before temptation ever comes down our street. If you spend time reading His word daily, He will inform you of the devils next move. If you find yourself constantly reading scriptures on adultery or sexual sin and situations, or if you begin to hear a lot of preaching and teaching on the topic then you should perk up, wake up and gird up your loins because sexual temptations are brewing and coming your way.

The temptation always comes before a big move of God in your life. The devil tries to come in and distract you so that he can get you off the path of your blessings. When God begins to deal with you on sexual sin, start fasting and meditating on the scriptures that God's placing before you so that you can humble yourself and not give in to the flesh. I understand lust and how it gravitates to you like a magnet especially if you're vulnerable but you must prepare in advance.

God knows you want your husband and the devil does to. The enemy sets up a plan to try and copycat God's plan. The good news is that if the devil is cooking up something, which we know he is, then God has finished the perfect meal. It's already done for us. Don't fall for the imitation. It might look like the real thing and it might smell like it to, but God has the final check. Take that thing to God to examine it. God created the perfect guy for you, so if you bring a counterfeit before Him, of course He knows that's not the one and He'll let you know. Throughout the entire process, God will give you red flags.

Don't ignore the signs because you're too desperate to wait a little longer. Wait on God for His absolute best. Your body belongs to God. Give it to Him as a living sacrifice, Holy and acceptable to Him which is your reasonable service according to Roman 12:1. If you have fallen, repent and get back up. Don't dwell on your failures but trust God from this moment on for your future. Learn from your mistakes, don't repeat them but use them to better someone else. Remember the whole point of the traps of the devil is to steal, kill and destroy. Your husband is to close, put down the bait and wait.

DAY FIFTEEN

Get A Grip On Your Finances

Prepare thy work without, and make it fit for thyself in the field; and afterwards build thine house.

Proverbs 24:27

If you don't have your finances in order by knowing how to budget and use self- control with your spending, now is the time. It's time for you to face this giant and slay it once and for all. Not only does your body belong to God, but your money does too. God desires to bless you. He wants to increase your finances so that you can live more comfortably, be a blessing to your children and to others. But you have to act responsibly and stop foolish spending. When God knows that you are ready an accountable for financial promotion, He'll increase you.

Are you constantly crying out to God because you don't have enough to pay your bills? Are you tired of living from check to check? Are you spending money on clothes, getting your hair done and eating out and now you need a miracle to pay your electric bill? If you've answered yes to any of these questions, it's time for a financial transformation. You have to make up your mind to stop wasting your money, grow up and walk in wisdom. Get yourself ready for your husband. You are asking God to give you a man with money, who has his own business. A man that's financial stable. Well do you think that your future husband is praying for a wife who can't keep a

dollar in her pocket? Un, un. I don't think so Queen. Get your finances in order.

    First of all, God has given you everything you need to increase with, but if you are blinded by the frustration of being broke and living in poverty because of your lack of self-control then you can't see clearly the way out. God supplies all your need, but you are overspending and can't see God's provision and you blame God for your lack of self-control. Stop looking at others comparing yourself to them or trying to keep up with them. Stop giving in to your flesh and surrender your money to God. Humble yourself so that He can exalt you in your finances.

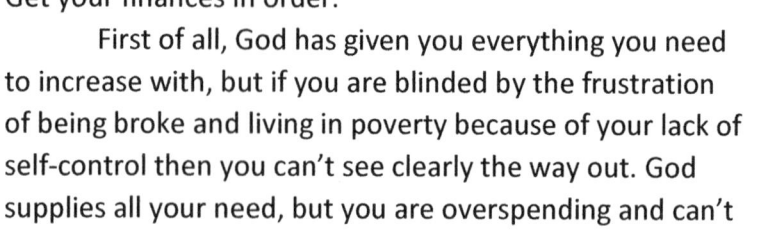

    God is calling you to fast your money. Get before the LORD God and ask Him to help you set up a budget and no matter what stick with it. Once you get the plan from God. Only spend money on the set days that you've planed and fast spending money on any other day. Do this for 40 days and continue until it becomes a habit. God has gifted you and the gift will make room for you, but it starts with taking care of what you have now. Pay your tithes and give your offerings as God lead you. Don't curse your money by not giving to God first.

Bring ye all the tithes into the storehouse, that there may be meat in mine house, and prove me now herewith, saith the LORD of hosts, if I will not open you the windows of heaven, and pour you out a blessing, that there shall not be room enough to receive it. And I will rebuke the devourer for your sakes, and he shall not destroy the fruits of your ground; neither shall your vine cast her fruit before the time in the field, saith the LORD of hosts.

Malachi 3:10-11

When you put God first, He will bless the work of your hands. Get ready for increase.

The LORD shall command the blessing upon thee in thy storehouses, and in all that thou settest thine hand unto; and he shall bless thee in the land which the LORD thy God giveth thee.

Deuteronomy 28:8

SIXTEEN

Stop Procrastination

Boast not thyself of tomorrow; for thou knowest not what a day may bring forth.

Proverbs 27:1

Tomorrow, tomorrow, tomorrow. I'll do it tomorrow. Does this sound like you? Wake up and get started on your dreams. Wake up and start losing weight and get your health together. Wake up and start that business. Wake up and get your life right with God. Wake up and start doing whatever it is you know you've been putting off for too long. Your life is but a vapor. Do you want to die and not accomplish any of your dreams? Do you want to stay overweight forever? Do you want to stay broke forever? Do you want your future husband to see you the way you are now? If not, get up, get out and do something different.

Now is the time to take a step towards your future. You are on your way to tomorrow rather you do something toward your dreams and goals or not. The question is "*What do you want to see when you reach your future?"* The answer to the question is in what you're doing today. If you are sick and tired of where you are, then take action going in a different direction. Turn around and go the opposite way from where you are headed. What are you expecting from God? Are you expecting promotion, prosperity, favor, opportunity? What are you believing God for? Do you really believe that God wants to bless you beyond measure? Do you believe that God will bring you to multitudes of people and use you in an amazing way? What has God promised to do in your life? Now what are you doing to prepare yourself for what you're expecting God to do in your life?

What are you waiting for and who are you waiting on? Are you sitting around waiting for everything to be perfect before you start? Are you waiting on your husband to come before you get started? Are you waiting on your finances to be right? Are you waiting until the right people come? If you are waiting on circumstances and situations to change before you get started then you would not be ready when the opportunity presents itself, therefore you won't get the opportunity.

OK, just say you were fat and out of shape and God kept dealing with you about your health and your weight but you kept putting it off. One day you were invited by a friend to an event but because you didn't feel comfortable going because of your weight, you didn't go. Your future husband was there but you didn't know it and now you missed the opportunity to meet him because you were not at the right place at the right time. Get ready now so that when the opportunity presents itself, you won't be getting ready, you will be ready.

SEVENTEEN

Stop Being Lazy

A little sleep, a little slumber, A little folding of the hands to rest; So shall your poverty come like a prowler, And your need like an armed man.

Proverbs 24:33-34

Everything you're believing God for is on the other side of that thing that you are too lazy to do. You quote scriptures, you make your daily confessions, you go to church and believe God for greatness, but the one thing you won't do is work. You got to move. You got to take action. I remember I use to go to the mailbox everyday believing God for a check, but guess what? No check ever came. After a while God blessed us with rental property because we took action. One day I went to the mail box and look and behold "A Check" with my name on it.

One of our renters was on a program that helped pay her rent and the check came in the mail every month. When I picked up the check, I heard the Holy Spirit say, *"See, now you've done something to generate a check."* At first I was looking for a check and had done nothing to produce one. So why was I expecting a check for doing nothing? I call it lazy faith. We want something from God, but don't want to work for it. It's deception. Because the Bible says that faith without works is dead. So if you are believing God for something and you aren't mixing action with your faith, then you are not really believing God. If you know God said that He was going to bless you with a business, what actions are you taking toward the promise? The key is seeking God for guidance and direction through fasting and prayer. Once you get a plan then do whatever He says to do.

     For instance; If you know God said he's going to bless you with your husband, prepare for it. Get up and work out. Learn how to cook. Get your money in order. Stretch yourself. Get out of the box. Do more than normal. Get around family and friends that are productive and glean from them. If you are lazy, you'll always be less than average. Whatever you have to do to get ready, do it because surely the blessings are on the way.

EIGHTEEN

Build Your Empire Queen

She considers a field and buys it;
From her profits she plants a vineyard.

Proverbs 31:16

Where's your focus? Are you so focused on getting married that you are stuck and can't move forward? God hasn't made a mistake. He has you exactly where He wants you to be and where you need to be. If you needed to be married at this point in your life, you would have been. You are in a place of destroying the old and rebuilding the new. God has you under construction and He's doing a new thing in your life, beginning with a new you.

This time of singleness is ordained by God. He wants to spend quality time with you. He wants to show you who you are and what you can do. He wants you to know that you don't need what or who you thought you needed in order to make it through life. God wants you to see how great you are and the mighty things that you can accomplish without depending on others. That husband that you think you need in order to build your dreams, your ministry, your businesses, you don't need him. The man you think you need to make you whole, God is telling you that you don't need him. You only need God. God and God alone, makes you whole. You are on the verge of breaking new ground. You are a great women of valor. You are not alone. God is your 1st Husband and He will cover you in all that you do. He'll walk with you and teach you and direct you in the right way. He'll never let you down. Fall in love with Him. Give Him your all.

If you are constantly thinking about your future husband until it destroys your focus, attitude and altitude, you've made an idol out of him and all idols must come down. God will have no other gods before Him. God promised you that He would give you a husband, if you really believe God, then act like it. Get busy serving God and put Him first in all that you do and when the time is right, God will gather you and your future mate together. Right now it's time to build up your body, spirit, soul and wealth. Build your empire Queen!

NINETEEN

Naked and Unashamed

And they were both naked, the man and his wife, and were not ashamed.

Genesis 2:25

Imagine your life as a mirror and in the mirror every area of your life is exposed for your future husband to see. If he looked in the area of your body would you be ashamed? If he looked into your spirit, would you hold your head down? If he looked at your finances, would you want to turn away and run? If he looked at your thought pattern, are there any unhealthy or unclean thoughts that that would shock him? What about your housekeeping, would you want him to see the way you take care of your home? Do you keep a clean or dirty house? Do you take care of the kids? What about your mouth? Would you be afraid for him to hear the words that you speak over yourself, your kids, your finances, your life and maybe even him? Wow, what a mirror!

Does any area of your life embarrass you because you know you are not making any effort to change? This chapter is not to make you feel inadequate, but to open your eyes so that you can come clean and be real with yourself. God wants you to acknowledge Him in every area of your life and to trust that He can and will help you fix all the broken pieces. He does not want you to be ashamed. He wants you to allow Him to help you so that you can tell others about His mercy and grace. He wants you to show others the love of God through your transformation.

The man that God is preparing you for will love you just the way you are. But the problem is, it's not his job to fix you. It's God's job to make you whole and to prepare you. We must stop expecting people to fix us. They are not capable of doing that. God is the creator and He knows how to put you back together again.

The point that I am making is that if you take this time and work on you, eventually you'll be able to look in the mirror and see yourself exactly the way God sees you, *"bad to the bone"* and *"Built like a brick."* Then God can bring you to your husband and you'll be ready baby, in every area of your life, naked and unashamed!

TWENTY

Guard Your Heart

Keep thy heart with all diligence; for out of it are the issues of life.

Proverbs 4:23

What are you listening to? What are you watching on TV? Who are you hanging around? The reason I asked these questions is because it's vital to the guarding of your heart. The things that you listen to plays an important role in the area of your emotions. Are you listening to love songs? Songs that feed your flesh and make you desperately want to be around a man, dating him, having sex with him and doing lustful things. Are you watching movies that make you want to be married so that you can legally kiss and make love? Are you hanging around women that are married and all they talk about *is "My husband this and my husband that"* and how good the marriage is, and it's making you impatient for your God-given mate?

Truth be told, the woman and her husband probably can't stand one another, don't sleep in the same bed and on their way to divorce court. And behind closed doors you're praying for a marriage just like theirs, not even realizing what you are praying for, which is a failed marriage. Are you hanging around women who are desperate for a husband? Even if you don't realize it, it's triggering desperation in you as well. What you listen to, watch on TV and who you hang around plays a major role in your emotions. The trick of the enemy is to get your heart so full of junk that you'll begin to say what's in your heart so that eventually you'll have the things you say, which would be contrary to the will of God for you.

Guard your heart. If you don't you'll eventually marry the wrong man out of desperation and insecurity. Most people settle for less because their heart is not in the right place with God. They fall off track because of impatience and find themselves making choices out of a heart that's full with everything else but God. We must turn off everything that feeds the flesh. The Bible teaches us that we shall reap what we sow. It also tells us that if we sow to the flesh we will reap corruption.

God wants you to have a marriage full of love and a match made in heaven. His will for you is to bring to earth the exact picture of you both that He has in heaven. Lust is of the devil and if you marry someone out of a lustful heart, your marriage won't be built on the right foundation. As soon as trouble comes, the house will fall down. The key to a successful marriage is to "*Wait on God.*" Trust in His ability to make it happened, not yours.

Trust in His arranged marriage for you. God knows what's best for you and in due season, it will happen if you *wait on God.*

TWENTY-ONE

Flat Lined

Now go and attack Amalek, and utterly destroy all that they have, and do not spare them. But kill both man and woman, infant and nursing child, ox and sheep, camel and donkey."

1 Samuel 15:3

It's time out for playing around with people of your past, unhealthy thoughts, bad attitudes, fleshly ideas, sin and anything that God has told you to get rid of. Destroy those thoughts. Let go of those so called friends. Walk away from that ungodly relationship that continuously try to trip you up, pull you under and leaves you miserable every time. Stop breathing life into those dead things.

God didn't say to put them to sleep and wake them when convenient for you. He didn't say run back to it when you hear it calling your name. He didn't say park it in the garage until you are ready to drive it again. He said to ***"Kill It."*** Demolish that toxic waste. It's poison and will contaminate you and eventually kill you and your destiny. Anything that God told you to let go of and you allow it to remain, it will suck the life right out of you like a leech. Its sucking away at your blood, literally killing you alive. It's designed to kill you. Stop pacifying blood suckers. Purpose in your heart that your future is much more important than those things. Destroy those bad thoughts and attitudes. Stop rehearsing the mistakes of your past and release the guilt and shame. If you know there are some things in your life that God told you to let go of, make a U-turn right now and go in the right direction.

Don't be like Saul in the Bible. God told him to kill all the Amalekites. Saul killed the ones he wanted to kill and kept alive the ones that he thought was valuable and convinced himself that he obeyed God fully. If we don't destroy the things that God is commanding us to, it will be a thorn in the flesh. Flat Line it and never give life to it again, you know what *"IT"* is. Tell it *"Good Bye."* Your future is too big and you have too much to live for to stay in the grave with the dead.

then you shall drive out all the inhabitants of the land from before you, destroy all their engraved stones, destroy all their molded images, and demolish all their high places;

Numbers 33:52

But if you do not drive out the inhabitants of the land from before you, then it shall be that those whom you let remain shall be irritants in your eyes and thorns in your sides, and they shall harass you in the land where you dwell. Moreover it shall be that I will do to you as I thought to do to them.'-Number 33:55-56

*They served their idols,
Which became a snare to them.*

Psalms 106:36

Do not be deceived: "Evil company corrupts good habits."

1 Corinthians 15:33

For the weapons of our warfare are not carnal but mighty in God for pulling down strongholds, casting down arguments and every high thing that exalts itself against the knowledge of God, bringing every thought into captivity to the obedience of Christ, and being ready to punish all disobedience when your obedience is fulfilled.

2 Corinthians 10:4-6

TWENTY-TWO

LORD Help Me I'm Lonely

Have I not commanded you? Be strong and of good courage; do not be afraid, nor be dismayed, for the LORD your God is with you wherever you go."

Joshua 1:9

Believe me when I tell you that I've experienced loneliness the majority of my life. I always felt as though some man would make that loneliness go away. I always kept a man in my life, I can't recall ever being fulfilled. Even though being in a relationship numbed my emotions of being by myself, it didn't take away the loneliness. I gave my life to Jesus when I was 7 years old and back slid probably the next day. The first time I had sex was at the age of 12 and I continued using sex to try and fill that void of loneliness.

Sex doesn't cure loneliness nor does it make a man want to be with you. If a man wants you, sex is the furthest thing from his mind. The most important thing that he's thinking of is *"How can I take care of her."* If he's not thinking that, you are not the one. Let's just be honest at least with ourselves. Praise God, He spared my life and gave me another chance to return back to Him at the age of 25. I gave my life to Jesus and immediately I wanted to get married so that I could make things right before God in my home. At the time, my ex-husband and I were living together and our first child together was 6 months old.

I begin talking to him about marriage and the silence from his end cut my heart like a knife. This man did not want to marry me. I'd been with him for three years. Cooking for him, washing his clothes, having his baby and none of those things convinced him to marry me. I told him that if he did not want to marry me, he had to go. Long story short, he left. It wasn't a month later that he asked me to marry him. We got married and all the opposite of heaven broke loose.

I should have waited on God. Because I spent 20 years in a marriage that words could not come close to express how lonely I was. If I had not falling in love with Jesus, I know I would have ruined my life trying to find love elsewhere. The loneliness that you are feeling is not because you want or need a husband, it's because you have placed your value in having a significant other.

Look, God wants you to understand that He is your everything. Your value is to be placed in Him and no one else. Having a spouse or boyfriend or anyone else does not signify your worth. Take this time to get to know Jesus and who He really is. Find out how much you really mean to Him and how much He truly loves and cares for you. No man can ever love you as much as He does and no one can replace Him. God has someone special for you, not to make you, but to compliment you. As long as God is with you, you are never alone. Married or not, until you understand God's purpose in your life, you'll always feel lonely, empty and a void.

TWENTY-THREE

Bigger Than You Think

"For My thoughts are not your thoughts,
Nor are your ways My ways," says the LORD.
"For as the heavens are higher than the earth,
So are My ways higher than your ways,
And My thoughts than your thoughts.

Isaiah 55:8-9

The blessing that God has prepared for you is so much bigger than you could have ever dreamed of. Your imagination could not explore such greatness. The doors that are opening for you will blow your mind. The most amazing news is that God has the perfect mate for you in position to walk through those doors with you. As a matter of fact, he is one of those miracle doors. You've watched others receive blessing after blessing for such a long time and now it's your turn.

It's your turn to receive your new husband, your new houses, your new cars, your new businesses and ministries. It's your time and season and your blessings are all on the way. God has been using all the struggles and tribulations to prepare you for such greatness. You had to wait. You had to go through everything that you have suffered because of the level of responsibility that God is about to trust you with. The reason it took so long for your breakthrough is because of the magnitude of what you are about to receive. It's bigger than you think.

God said that His thoughts are not your thoughts and His ways are not your ways. His ways and thoughts are higher than yours. So whatever you are thinking right now, God's doing it on a greater level. God is about to enlarge your territory according to 1 Chronicles 4:10. He's about to enlarge the place of your tents and stretch out the curtains of your dwellings according to Isaiah 54:2. God is doing it big. He has not forgotten about you, He just had a much larger order to make and to deliver to you. It's coming. It's coming. It's coming.

Don't be afraid, though it's huge and more than you have ever experienced before, God got you and He will help you carry your blessings. God knows you are ready now. He knows that you are going to do the right thing with His gifts to you. He knows that you will love your husband right. You are in position for your biggest blessings ever.

TWENTY-FOUR

He's Asking About You

Boaz asked his young servant who was foreman over the farm hands, "Who is this young woman? Where did she come from?"

Ruth 2:5 (Message)

If you can hold on in the hard times and stay on the path, trusting that God will restore, God will restore. You may have lost a lot but the pay back is so awesome that you'll remember the pain no more. The joy of God's restoration will leave you speechless and every tear that you've shed over the lost can't compare to the laughter that awaits.

There's a story in the Bible, in the book of Ruth, where a woman by the name of Naomi lost it all. She left her home town of Bethlehem and went to Moab with her husband and two sons because of the famine in Bethlehem. During the process of the stay, she lost her husband and her two sons. She was very depressed and bitter. She made up her mind to return back to her home land. Both of her sons had married, Ruth, one of her daughter-in- laws purposed in her heart to follow Naomi where ever she went. Ruth had no clue what she was about to enter into. Ruth lost her husband. She left the only home she had ever known to follow a God that was unknown to her and her culture. She forsook everything and in forsaking everything she gained it all. Ruth did not let loss cause her to get off the path. She stayed on the right path and entered into a field owned by Boaz, a very rich man. Boaz took one look at her and asked, *"Who is she?"* God had given her favor with the right person.

All it takes is favor with the right person to shift you from one level to the next. She went from gleaning in the field behind reapers to owning the field because she eventually became his wife. God has allowed you to get into trouble so that He can show you off. He's allowed you to enter the right field to work so that pretty soon it will be yours. It may not seem as though things are working out in your favor, but God is working things out for you on your behalf, behind the scenes.

Some body is asking God, *"Who is she?"* Because God is revealing you to your future husband. God is stirring up his desire for you. He's praying day and night for you. His desire is for you. God wants you to have the best. He has the right person waiting to cater to you, love you and treat you like the Queen that you are. God has a king for you and not a little boy. In the past you have reached so low because you didn't think that you deserved any better, but God has, through this season of singleness, built your confidence and now you are ready to reach higher and get all that you deserve.

TWENTY-FIVE

Patience for the Promise

But let patience have her perfect work, that ye may be perfect and entire, wanting nothing.

James 1:4

Are you facing anything in your life today that seems to be too much to handle? Is the pressure mounting up minute by minute? Do you feel all alone in your trials and tribulations wondering *"Where's God?"* I am here to tell you that no matter what you are dealing with, God's there with you. I want to share something with you that you may not like. The truth of the matter is, God ordained this trial. The attacks that you are experiencing are sent by God.

The pain and heartache that you're encountering is a set up by God. I know it's hard to believe that a loving God would send such pain and anguish on you. I know you thought it was the enemy but it's for a purpose. The Bible tells us to count it all joy when we are faced with various trials. God does nothing without purpose. There's purpose in your pain. You are in a place of birthing something new.

But in order to bring forth something new, something old must die. Is it your attitude that God is trying to kill? Could it be an old relationship that God is telling you to let go of? It really doesn't matter what you are trying to hold on to that God wants dead, believe me, after these trials you'll be screaming for God to take that thing away from you. The suffering and pain is the cup of the LORD.

You must drink of it. There's no way around it. God has a plan for your life. He has promised you great things and He always keeps His promises. But before the promise is the test. Will you allow God to use you? Are you willing to drink of this cup crying, *"Lord please let this cup pass, but not my will but Your will be done?"*

God promised Abraham a son. God gave Abraham the promise which was Isaac, then tested him to see if he loved the promise more than God. What has God promised you? Whatever your promise is, this is the process. Trust God to bring you through this test. He will bring you through and deliver into your hands everything He's promised you. Hold on to the promise.

TWENTY-SIX

Renew Your Mind

And do not be conformed to this world, but be transformed by the renewing of your mind, that you may prove what is that good and acceptable and perfect will of God.

Romans 12:2

Are you ready to rise? Are you ready to come out of the place of complacency? Are you ready to walk in your purpose? Are you ready for the blessing God has for you? Are you mentally in a place to receive your miracles? In order for you to rise above where you are to where God is taking you, you must change your mind. Take some time out to evaluate your thoughts. If you think you are not worthy, you are limited and keeping God's best from ever reaching your life.

Proverbs 23:7 says "As a man thinks in his heart, so is he". What are you thinking? Do you think that you are always going to fail? Do you think that you could never be or do great out of the box things? Do you think that bad things always happen to you? Do you think you'll never have more than enough? Do you think you'll always be stuck? What do you think about all the time? Do you think positive things or negative things? Examine your life and the position that you are in. Are you happy with your life? Are you in the blessed place that you know you should be in right now? Are you achieving great accomplishments on the level that you know you desire to be on? I know that I am asking you a lot of questions, but it's a must.

You need to take self- inventory so that you can evaluate your current situation and make the proper adjustments. This is your responsibility, you must rise up and deal with it. Get in God's word daily and change the way you see yourself. If you read and meditate on the word of God, it will change you. It will change your perception and perspective on how you see things.

Renew your mind by allowing God's word to build you up in faith. If you believe that you can do all things through Christ that strengthens you, then you can. If you believe that you are blessed coming in and blessed going out, then you will be. If you believe that no weapon formed against you shall prosper, then it won't. Success is formed in the mind. Your creativity is in your mind.

If your mind is filled with all doubt, unbelief and fear, there's no room for creativity to flow. This is a job that only you can do. Start reading the Bible daily and apply it to your life. Make a list of confessions that you want to see happen in your life and confess them daily until you see them come to pass. It's a process but well worth it. Your future husband will be very happy that you made the investment.

So here's what I want you to do, God helping you: Take your everyday, ordinary life—your sleeping, eating, going-to-work, and walking-around life—and place it before God as an offering. Embracing what God does for you is the best thing you can do for him. Don't become so well-adjusted to your culture that you fit into it without even thinking. Instead, fix your attention on God. You'll be changed from the inside out. Readily recognize what he wants from you, and quickly respond to it. Unlike the culture around you, always dragging you down to its level of immaturity, God brings the best out of you, develops well-formed maturity in you.

Romans 12:1-2 (Message)

TWENTY-SEVEN

Be Still

Be still, and know that I am God; I will be exalted among the nations, I will be exalted in the earth!

Psalm 46:10

One of the hardest things to do in life is to *"Be Still"*. We as people and especially women always want to help out. Our nature by right is to help. But we somehow think that our job to help God. God said in Genesis 2:18 that it's not good for man to be alone, I will make him a helper comparable to him. I DON'T see anywhere in the Bible where He said that He will have the woman do it.

God is working on this right here. Your job is to be still and trust God. The more you try to put your handy work into the job, you're ruining the project and in order for God to fix what's damaged it takes more time. This battle is not yours so you don't need to fight in it. It doesn't matter how bad the fight looks. I know it seems as though you are losing and your enemy is winning, but don't lose focus on who your enemy is fighting against. The fight is fixed. Of course if you were the one fighting then you would have a reason to be afraid, but you are not. God is the one fighting on your behalf and He has never lost a battle. When you feel worried and agitated in your waiting process, remind yourself of the promise and who promised it. If you think on good things, then you'll be able to wait in faith.

You have to cast your cares on God the moment they enter your mind. If not you will find yourself meditating on when, where and how, trying to figure things out. This becomes a problem because God probably hasn't told you when He's going to do it, how it's going to get down or who He's going to use to do it. So to be safe, just calm down and relax, trust Him and know that it will get done and that it's going to work out in your favor.

Finally, brethren, whatever things are true, whatever things are noble, whatever things are just, whatever things are pure, whatever things are lovely, whatever things are of good report, if there is any virtue and if there is anything praiseworthy—meditate on these things.

Philippians 4:8

TWENTY-EIGHT

Girl, Loose Him & Let Him Go

And he who had died came out bound hand and foot with grave clothes, and his face was wrapped with a cloth. Jesus said to them, "Loose him, and let him go."

John 11:44

I can remember as a teen I looked for love in all the wrong places and believe me I found all the wrong boys. We spend too much of our time and lives looking for somebody to love us and eventually finding another heart ache. We dig up dead graves and expect something living to come out of them. Are you in a bad relationship? Are you holding on to someone that God told you to release?

Are you praying for a man to be the One knowing that God already told you he wasn't? Are you in an adulterous affair with someone else's husband? If you have answered yes to any one of these questions, girl you need to release that man and let him go. You are not blocking him from his destiny, you are blocking yourself.

You are hindering your blessing and drowning yourself in quick sand. Check yourself. Realize that it's not about you and it's not your choice. You have prayed and asked God to take the wheel and if God is the driver, He's going to make some stops. He will pull over and put some people out of the car. If you expect to reach your destination you much stop and drop off the dead weight. Forget about the shame of your past and the mistakes you've made. Forgive yourself and move forward. Keep your eyes on Jesus, the Driver.

Therefore we also, since we are surrounded by so great a cloud of witnesses, let us lay aside every weight, and the sin which so easily ensnares us, and let us run with endurance the race that is set before us, looking unto Jesus, the author and finisher of our faith, who for the joy that was set before Him endured the cross, despising the shame, and has sat down at the right hand of the throne of God.

Hebrews 12:1-2

God has so much more in store for you. Girl, let that joker go. It's an imitation sent by the devil. Ask God to expose the enemy and He will. Isaiah 2:22 says "*Sever yourselves from such a man, Whose breath is in his nostrils; For of what account is he?*" Don't put your trust in no man, they will disappoint you every time. Get out of that thing. Run for your life and your future and don't look back.

You have tried and tried to do it your way and it never seems to turn out in your favor. You have given your heart to the wrong men for too long and It has almost ruined you. You are so use to bad relationships that it's your normal. Though you are uncomfortable in the bad relationships, yet you remain. Let it go. Let go of your past. Let go of your judgment. Let go of your preconceived way of viewing things. Your mind needs to be renewed and transformed. The way you've done things have built invisible walls that's keeping the best life has to offer you, out. Those walls must come down. God is doing a new thing and you better get on board. While you are releasing your past, release yourself to live, learn new things and most of all learn to love yourself.

TWENTY-NINE

Watch & Pray

Watch and pray, lest you enter into temptation. The spirit indeed is willing, but the flesh is weak."

Matthew 26:41

Always remember that temptation is just right around the corner. Whenever you purpose in your heart to seek after God through fasting, prayer and spending time in His word, expect the devil to rise from the grave. He's sliding somewhere in the grass just waiting to make his move. He's out to poison God's purpose for your life. The enemy is going to do everything in his power to try and get you to do the opposite of what God is telling you to do.

If God is telling you to wait for marriage, the devil is telling you to get married now. He knows that your flesh doesn't want to wait but it wants right now gratification so he offers an imitation of the promise. Most of the time God will have us do things that we don't want to do like wait, fast, pray and forgive.

Jesus, in the garden of Gethsemane had to pray in order to fulfill the purpose of God. If Jesus had to pray to accomplish the will of God, so do we all. Keep your eyes open and your ears perked up, and stay focused. The test is always before the testimony. The enemy wants to ruin your testimony. He does not want you to give God the glory for gracefully bringing you through the fire without smelling like smoke. Fasting is so vital. It's a must.

    It's your weapon of warfare. Fasting keeps your flesh under submission because it weakens its power. The more food you eat, the stronger your flesh. The less food you eat the weaker your flesh. The power is not in what you eat and don't eat, the power is in the sacrifice for spiritual reasons. Fasting is the key when you are doing it out of obedience to God. God has the keys to the Kingdom and He has promised to give them to us.

    Fasting is an amazing key to open powerful doors. Whenever God tells you to fast, it's for a reason. If you want to win the battle, obey God's plan.

THIRTY

What Are You Waiting On?

When He had stopped speaking, He said to Simon, "Launch out into the deep and let down your nets for a catch."

Luke 5:4

What are you waiting on to get started with your God-given assignments? Are you waiting on your mate? Are you waiting for somebody to come along to pick you up and carry you off into the sunset? Are you living or just surviving watching others pass you by? What are you Waiting on? Who are you waiting on? The only person that you should be waiting on is Jesus and the truth is, Jesus is waiting on you. He has already given you the plan, but you are afraid because you think you have to do it alone.

You are not alone, God is with you and He has already made a way for you. You must stop making excuses and get going. Time is not waiting on you. The clock is ticking rather you do something or not. You got to get going or life will leave you behind. You don't have to start and finish the project in one day, but you must do something toward your dreams. God is with you. He will never leave you or forsake you. He knows that you are afraid that's why He promised to be there with you. The mantle and assignment on your life is major but God has you covered. He will send the right people at the right time to assist you.

God gave Moses an assignment to go and bring His people out of bondage from the land of Egypt to the land of Canaan. Moses looked at the task and immediately tried to get out of it. God wanted to show Himself strong through Moses and He wants to so Himself strong through you.

And He said, "My Presence will go with you, and I will give you rest."

Exodus 33:14

God promised that He will be with you and He is the one working the miracles. The fear that you are experiencing comes from the fact that you think it's all about you. This has nothing to do with you, you are just a vessel that He desires to work through. I's not by might or by power but by His Spirit. (Zechariah 4:6). You don't have to defend your call all you have to do is get up and go. You may have to go alone without anyone but God, but as long as God is there with you, you're set. As you get going you will meet all the amazing, hardworking, committed and faithful people that's orchestrated by God to walk along this journey and work together with you. You'll never met them if you don't go.

THIRTY-ONE

Stop Complaining

Now when the people complained, it displeased the LORD; for the LORD heard it, and His anger was aroused. So the fire of the LORD burned among them, and consumed some in the outskirts of the camp.

Numbers 11:1

There's so many things that we can find ourselves murmuring and complaining about. But complaining makes a loud statement that says "I Don't Trust God" and I am not grateful for what He has done already". God has done so much for you and instead of looking at your problems you need to fix your eyes on the problem Solver.

God has never let you down. His track record is sure. Why would you doubt Him now? Complaining is a destroyer. The more you complain the more you will remain in the mess that you are in. God allowed you to go through the trouble for a reason. He will use every situation and circumstance to grow you up not to destroy you. The enemy always wants for you to focus on your problems and develop the "Woe is me" syndrome. He will continue to drop thoughts of ungratefulness in your mind so that you can find reasons to complain. We must guard our minds. Keep the word of faith before you continuously especially when you are going through trials.

Build your faith by spending time reading the Bible and listening to faith teachers and motivational leaders. You are under attack, but you must understand how to fight back in order to win. When we were in the world, we fought our own battles, with our mouths and sometimes physically. We said some horrible things, some too bad to repeat. We did whatever we had to in order to win the fight. Now that we are in the Kingdom of God, our fight is a spiritual fight. We can't hit the devil with our fist. We can't spit on the devil or throw anything at him.

We must fight our battles God's way. We must praise God no matter what we are facing. We must walk by faith and declare what we want and not what we have. We must trust God and thank Him in advance for what we are believing Him for. We win every time we do it God's way. You will come through this. Trust and believe God will turn it around for you if you hang on in there.

THIRTY-TWO

One More Chance

David said to Nathan, "I have sinned against the LORD." And Nathan said to David, "The LORD also has put away your sin; you shall not die.

2 Samuel 12:13

God is about to give you another chance. Whatever you've messed up in the past, be it a relationship, business opportunity or ministry, it doesn't matter because He is giving you another chance. As I write this, I am reminded of David and his encounter with Bathsheba. David saw how beautiful the woman was and he just had to have her knowing that she was married.

He called the woman to him, had sex with her and got her pregnant. Once he found out that the woman had become pregnant, he tried to manipulate things to get her husband to come home, make love to his wife so that he would think that the baby was his. Unfortunately, his plan failed and eventually he got her husband killed, brought the woman to him and married her. You would expect God to say something right away, but God said nothing until the opportune time. God sent the Prophet Nathan to expound on the matter. Nathan gave a parable about an unjust situation and David was angry and wanted the man in the story put the death.

Imagine David's shock when he found out that the man in the parable was him. God told David that the child that Bathsheba was carrying would die. David fasted and prayed in order to save the child's life. The baby eventually died, but God's grace is so amazingly incredible. God gave David another chance and he and Bathsheba had another child and God called him Solomon which means peace. God restored peace back in David's life.

What mistakes have you made that you feel as though there's no way God can and will fix such mess? What is it that has you all discombobulated and has stolen your peace? Look up and see God's mercy and grace all over that thing. God is about to give you another chance. It may not be the same thing but it will be another chance at that thing which was. Get ready for another chance.

THIRTY-THREE

Believe

Therefore I say to you, whatever things you ask when you pray, believe that you receive them, and you will have them.

Mark 11:24

Believing is very critical to receiving anything from God. The entire Bible is full of people who did not believe God and therefore they did not receive the promises of God. The problem with God's promises is things never look like what He says. God always calls things that are not as though they were according to Romans 4:17. He calls the things that does not exist as though they did.

The Bible talks about this very thing in the book of Genesis. He created the entire world with His Word. He spoke things into being. He spoke and said "Let there be light" and the Bible said the light appeared. Everything God created was brought forth from what was not visible. That's why it's so important to hold on to your faith. Hebrews 11:1 says "Now faith is the substance of things hoped for the evidence of things not seen." God does not owe us anything. Why would He play with your emotions?

God does not say things just to flatter you. Everything He allows in your life is for purpose. He's not wasting your time or His. Regardless of how big the word is that He's spoken over you, don't doubt what He says. Abraham was 100 years old and his wife was in her 90's and barren. God promised them a son. How on earth could this be? They both tried to figure out how this thing was going to work out. After trying to figure things out, Sarah came up with an idea to give her maid servant to Abraham as a concubine so that she could be the solution.

Eventually this thing caused problems in their home and Sarah's idea came back to mock her. Eventually God had to fix the mess they made. At the appointed time, God open Sarah's womb and she had a child from her own body just as God promised. No matter what you are facing today, trust God to bring forth everything He promised you. If you have any doubt, ask God to heal your unbelief. It's easy to get into a place of doubt when all obstacles are stacked against you. You must stay connected to God. Don't lose heart and don't give up.

THIRTY-FOUR

Forgive and Move On

"And whenever you stand praying, if you have anything against anyone, forgive him, that your Father in heaven may also forgive you your trespasses."

Mark 11:25

When you think about a situation where you were betrayed and hurt by someone you trusted, how does it make you feel? Is there anyone in your past that has caused you pain? Is there anyone's name that when you hear it causes you to cringe? Take a few minutes to reflect on issues in your past that you know you haven't been delivered from. Who are you in bondage to? I can remember a situation in my old church where certain people talked about me like a dog. It hurt me so bad. I was so angry and I wanted vindication. It seemed as though they were continuously being fruitful and blessed but I was confused and in captivity.

    I remember talking to God about this situation and I heard the LORD say to me that I was poisoned by the root of bitterness. I could not believe what I was hearing. I went before my Father God to tell Him about the hurt and pain those people cause me at that church and He tells me that I am poisoned by the root of bitterness. I was so hurt and I felt so betrayed by

God. I literally felt like God did not love me. I sat there on the couch trying to overcome my little feeling forsaken emotions. Eventually I came to myself and repented for allowing bitterness to control me and I faced my unforgiving self. I was so hurt and disappointed with myself for allowing such offense to control my life. I was broken and I needed God to fix me.

I needed to learn how to walk in forgiveness and love. I was the type pf person that always held on to hurt and pain. I was used to being rejected. I lived a lonely life because of the fear of being rejected. In my marriage I eventually built a wall around my heart so that the fiery darts that were thrown would not penetrate. The problem with the wall was that I locked true love out. I couldn't love with my whole heart and neither did I receive love to a certain point.

God does not want us spending our lives holding on to grudges. He wants us free from the traps of the enemy. Offense is a trap and it will cause you to never be able to move forward into greatness. The people that you think you are holding in your cave by not forgiving them, are not there. They are not in your cave, they are free, walking around in greatness. You are the only one stuck and can't break free. Let yourself go.

Ask God for help and deliverance. The reason why God has you looking in the mirror of bitterness is because you have some that you must let go of before you can be free to be the woman that God called you to be. God has a great husband and wonderful marriage and life for you, but you must let go of the offenses. Forgive and your Heavenly Father will forgive you. Don't kick, fight or try to play dead to the issue at hand just surrender your heart and watch God work.

THIRTY-FIVE

One Focus

For your Maker is your husband, The LORD of hosts is His name;
And your Redeemer is the Holy One of Israel;
He is called the God of the whole earth.

Isaiah 54:5

You are in this place of singleness for a reason. God has a plan. God loves you and He wants to spend quality time with you as His wife. You are God's one focus and at this point and time in your life you should only have One focus and that focus should be Jesus and how you can serve Him. Find out what He likes and how He wants you to please Him. He desires you to know Him and His ways. You need to forsake all thoughts of a man and focus your heart and your mind on Jesus and Him alone.

Shut down everything that distract you from being in love with Jesus. Purpose in your heart not to date are enter into new relationships with men at this point in your life. Shut it down. Go before the throne of grace and repent for neglecting God. Are you putting that person before God? Repent for making idols out of relationships. The reason why they are not lasting is because they are not ordained by God. The Bible says that God is a jealous

God. He knows where your heart is and how desperate you are to have a husband. You made a habit of going from one relationship to the next only to leave each relationship even more thirsty than you entered in. You are looking for a man to fulfill the void that you have.

  This time of being single is a time of restoration in your life. God wants to restore your heart, fill you with joy and heal you of all the pain and suffering. But how could He restore you if you are constantly running away from Him. He wants you to separate yourself from the dead relationship patterns that you've developed, that obviously does not work. I am not saying that it will be easy to get your heart in a place of surrender totally to God, but it's worth the push.

  Press into God. Fall in love with Him. Appreciate the doors that He shut. Rejoice in the fact that you can go to bed and rest at night because you trust Him enough to let go of all the foolishness that comes with flesh making decisions. Purpose in your heart to fall in love with God and wait patiently in His presence for Him to take you to another level which may or may not include a new husband. You have to be willing to be with God and God alone. Focus on Jesus and things above.

  Draw nigh unto God. Resist the devil and he will flee. Start putting God first and stop allowing the things of this world to take your attention off of Him. Once you make a vow to love Him and surrender all, your life will never be the same. You'll look at everything in your life in a new way.

THIRTY-SIX

Wake Up

*Arise, shine; For your light has come!
And the glory of the LORD is risen upon you.*

Isaiah 60:1

You may be in a place right now where you feel as if things are not moving in your favor. It may seem as though God is not working on your behalf. But I am here to tell you that you are favored by God. You may be in a pit right now, but just like Joseph, in your pit and prison, God has showered you with mercy and grace. Keep doing your best. Don't complain about being mistreated. Don't compare your circumstances to anyone else's.

Wake up and smell the favor. The devil Is trying to put you to sleep. Don't be dismayed at the attacks that are coming to try you. They are there for a divine purpose. I know it may seem as if everybody has forgotten about you even though you do everything you can to help others succeed and it makes you feel discouraged and sometimes angry. Wake up it's only a test. Will you give your best even when you are not getting anything in return? Are you going to go the extra mile even if you are unappreciated? Joseph gave his all. He went above and beyond while he was in Potiphar's house and when he was in prison. Joseph knew how to abound and to be abased. He did not let his situation change his character.

God is working on your character. He's using these things to make you walk in excellence regardless if it's not favorable conditions. Who cares what men think. Your job is to do all that you do to the glory and honor of God. And when the time is right, God will promote you. He will bring you before great men that will acknowledge your gifts and talents. He will bring you before people that will praise you for the work of your hands and as long as you give God all the glory, God will continue to promote you.

The Bible says that promotion does not come from the east nor the west but from God. He puts up one and cast down another. Don't listen to the enemy when he tells you that God has forgotten about you, he is a liar and can't tell the truth. Cast all your cares on God and trust Him.

Be sober, be vigilant; because your adversary the devil walks about like a roaring lion, seeking whom he may devour. Resist him, steadfast in the faith, knowing that the same sufferings are experienced by your brotherhood in the world.

1 Peter 5:8-9

THIRTY-SEVEN

Ready

*Preach the word! Be ready in season and out of season.
Convince, rebuke, exhort, with all longsuffering and teaching.*

2 Timothy 4:2

There's a saying that say's "When the student is ready, the teacher presents himself?" You don't have to wonder if you are ready or not. Your job is to get ready and when you are ready you'll know because the blessing will appear. Don't be afraid of missing any opportunities. As long as you are seeking God first and allowing Him to guide your footsteps, I promise you that you won't miss a beat. Even in some of your decision making, it may seem as though you made the wrong choice, and even if you did, God is going to work it all out for your good.

This is the time that you have been waiting on. You may not know when but just know that God is about to change your life forever. Your breakthrough has finally settled down and about to break-forth in your life. All while God has been working on you, He has been positioning your platform. He is about to present you to purpose. The world is going to see the glory but God is going to allow you to tell your story. I suggest that you get some waterproof mascara because tears will fall all over the place. God is about to allow you to meet back up with those tears that you shed for so long. Each tear has an assignment and now they are about to manifest.

Just look at the people throughout the Bible. The ones that God used in mighty ways suffered the most. And we all know that Jesus suffered greater than us all for us all, but look at His crown. Now who do you know that can be the Son and Father at the same time. WOW. Also just take a look throughout history of all the successful people and how they suffered only to accomplish great things in life that outlasted them. They are resting and were enjoying the benefits, such as electricity and airplanes. "Look at God". And if that's not enough, just look around you. Look at Tyler Perry, Oprah Winfrey, Joyce Myers, Paula White, Bishop T. D. Jakes.

I must tell you that this book has been birthed because God allowed Bishop T. D. Jakes to preach me through my pain, hurt, and suffering. God used him to help me understand my position in one of the hardest times of my life and to help me transition. God used him to show me His Exit Strategy". I had no one to talk to. God shut every door on every relationship and put me in the birthing potion and allowed Bishop to help me push. You too have a major assignment that is about to present itself. Connections that are about to take place. Business opportunities that are about to manifest. He is inducing your labor. Get ready and PUSH!

THIRTY-EIGHT

Return to God & Relax

So you, by the help of your God, return; Observe mercy and justice, And wait on your God continually.

Hosea 12:6

The first thing I would like to say is "How Great is Our God"? Our God is the One and only. He is Alpha and Omega. He is our Wonderful Counselor. He is The First and the Last. He is the Beginning and the End. He is everything that we need Him to be. He is our provider. The Psalmist David put it this way "I was young and now I am old, yet I have never seen the righteous forsaken nor his seed begging bread". God will never forsake you.

I know things happen that make us question God sometimes. But once we get out of our emotions we worship Him for who He is. Why do we allow ourselves to worry so easily about so many things? We worry about what we don't have and then turn around and worry about it once we get it. We're so easily distracted from His mercy and grace. God wants us to return to the place with Him that we once were. When we first got saved we were so in love and trusted in God totally. No one could move us from that place of rest and peace. Then some kind of way, we lost focus and started mixing our new way of life with fear. How could this have happened? We must return to the place of resting in Him. We need to go back to the place of seeking Him first. Matthew 6:33 says "Seek Ye first the Kingdom of God and His righteousness and all these things shall be added unto us." We are not to worry about food, clothing or anything else.

God is our Father and our provider. If we being evil know how to give good gifts to our children and want the very best for them, how much more does our heavenly Father want to take care of us? There is a conflict of trust going on. God is challenging us to return to the place of trusting Him without a shadow of doubt. A place of knowing that God will supply all of your needs according to His riches and glory. God wants us to return to a place of walking by faith with every step that we take. We are to know that God is with us though we don't see Him.

We need to get back to the place where His presence is so relevant in our lives. People should see the presence of God on your life and desire to know Him through your worship. How's your worship? How's your praise? Don't wait until God bring you the answers to your prayers to worship and or praise God. Worship and praise God for who He is and not only for what He does. Return back to that special place of rest and God will restore everything that was stolen from you.

THIRTY-NINE

Finish What You Started

Now finish the work, so that your eager willingness to do it may be matched by your completion of it, according to your means.

2 Corinthians 8:11 (NIV)

It's time to break the cycle of starting things and not finishing them. This is a bad habit to break, but you must break it. Take a look at all the projects that you started and ask God to show you which ones to complete, start working on it immediately. When you start something and do not finish, it blocks the flow of creativity in your life and it stops God from freely flowing through you. Jesus mother told the servants in John 2:5 "Whatever He tells you to do, do it". God is saying that very thing to you. If you want to see miracles in your life, do what He say's.

Do not be afraid. Don't worry if no one supports you. Do something daily toward that project. As you move forward, God will open doors. God will provide for you as you obey Him. Birth out the book, video, song, movie or whatever God has assigned you to do, it will make room for new projects. The flow will begin to move and new idea's will come forth. You will begin to do things that you never imagined. There is so many hidden talents and gifts wrapped up inside of you. God wants to dig up the hidden treasures. God has invested so much in you. He has gifted you with greatness and He expect's a return on His investment. This is critical. God did not gift you for you to bury your gifts and sleep on your talents.

He gave you the gifts to utilize so that you can build the kingdom of God. There's somebody out there that needs that thing that you are setting on. You must finish it. You don't have a choice. Your connections, blessings and major opportunities are all wrapped up in the things you won't finish. Who are you waiting on in order to finish? Apparently who every you are waiting on isn't coming.

Jesus is telling you to pick up your bed and walk. Get up and finish the work that He has called you to do. Let go of whatever hindered you and got you off track and pick up your book and write, pick up the mic and sing, go back and open up the church or start the ministry. No more excuses. This is your job to take care of. People are in need of what's planted inside you.

Water the thing and allow it to grow so that it can feed those that are hungry for God's provision provided through you. God will help you. He will finish the work He started in you. You are blazing an amazing trail. Encourage yourself and stay motivated.

being confident of this very thing, that He who has begun a good work in you will complete it until the day of Jesus Christ;

Philippians 1:6

FORTY

Ram in The Thicket

Then Abraham lifted his eyes and looked, and there behind him was a ram caught in a thicket by its horns. So Abraham went and took the ram, and offered it up for a burnt offering instead of his son.

Genesis 22:13

God is setting you up for a miracle. When I tell you that you are on the verge of a breakthrough and not a breakdown please believe me. God has your ram waiting on you. It will be everything that you prayed for. It might not come perfected but it has everything inside of it that you need. God is going to open your package right before your eyes and when He's done you'll know that it was nobody but God. When this test right here is done and complete, you are going to see a shift that will elevate you to a new dimension.

Your eye's can't even imagine the BIG blessing that's about to happen in your life. God has taken you through the hardest test that you've ever experienced before because He's about bless you in a way that you have never seen before. You may not understand what He's doing now, but you will pretty soon. Stay on the path. Press in and trust Him like you've never done before. Keep your eye's glued to God and His promises and don't give the enemy no time at all. The separation that you are going through right now is not to make you feel lonely, it's a call to draw closer to God. God wants to talk to you.

    He wants to share secrets with you and if He didn't separate you from your friends and or the ones whom you love to talk and listen to, then He could not get you in that secret closet with Him. The separation is temporary. When God finishes revealing things to you, He will restore relationships. It's just a matter of time.

    He has information about your future and plans and ideas to relay to you. You are in a new place and in this place you need new directions. He promised to lead and guide you in the right way. He has a new path for you to walk on and unless He strip you of the old, you could not contain the new. This is a new season, place and time for you. God is imparting a new anointing on your life and birthing you out to do new things for Him. The time is drawing close.

Notes

Made in the USA
Middletown, DE
17 March 2021